Water Into Wine
A Part of the Journey

Water Into Wine
A Part of the Journey

Empress Poetry

Niamani Inks
2015

First Printing: 2015

ISBN 978-0-578-17170-8

Niamani Inks

Brooklyn, NY 11226

Empress.poetry1@gmail.com

Cover by So Rich Graphix, Inc.

Sorichgraphix@gmail.com

Dedication

I was 21 when I lost the man who had been the modern day Jesus to me; the one who turned life's water into wine without me even realizing the miraculous things he had done to make sure all was well with me; MY FATHER.

My MOTHER has never been one to say, "We have no more wine" she would just squeeze all the grapes we had left; including the sour ones, to make sure our wine continued to flow. She has a way of adding sugar to the water so things always seem sweet. I am blessed to still have her in my life.

My Inspiration; given to me because God knows I need her. She is my Light, my fire and my desire.

My Village, a collective of blood relatives, strangers, loved ones and invested ones who stand as vessels filled with love at a depth that runs roots deep.

I aim to honor them on this journey

Acknowledgements

Special Thanks to:

Maya Layne
So Rich Graphix
Tashika Manderville
Mimi Spence
Eloise Mayers
Stephanie Pierre
Andrea Alleyne
Joyann Mulder
Patrick Fuller, Sr.
Jasmyn Cumberbatch
Negus Adeyemi
Stephanie Chase
Kwame Reina
The Inkwell Jazz and Comedy Café, Brooklyn, NY

Each of you have been special vessels in bringing this project to fruition. I Love you; God bless.

Foreword

Heart wrenching, bold and powerful are some of the words that describe Empress Poetry's new book "Water Into Wine; A Part of the Journey.'

Her journey of self-discovery offers a path to higher spiritual enlightenment that anyone who walks by faith could relate to. In these pages she provides readers with captivating anecdotes of her life experiences via fascinating essays, prose, and biblical excerpts. Pain and desolation scream out from the pages...often making one wonder will she experience the victory that she deserves?

Eventually she gains her crown but not without many trials and tribulations. She bares her soul with the hope that in revealing all she may help someone else to heal. She reminds us that in searching for complete perfection we often neglect or ignore the beauty and strengths that lie within us.

The only way that we can "turn water into wine" is by first accepting the taste, transparency and cleanliness of the water....to find that inner peace we must be at one with ourselves and understand that the journey to your true self is never without conflict. Self love, discipline, intuition, ambition, the ability to trust in your instincts and most importantly faith will guide you to where you need to be.

Stephanie F. Chase
Msc., B.A, Dip Ed. Asc., Miss Barbados World 2001/ Miss World Best Talent Winner

Preface

Water Into Wine; A Part of the Journey is a collection of my memories, thoughts, poetry and experiences. Using the scriptures as my footprints; I tell my story hoping that along the way the messages of encouragement & inspiration are received. It is our purpose to stay PRAYERFUL, GOD FAITHFUL, to LIVE, FIGHT & CELEBRATE LIFE!

Introduction

John 2:3-10

3. When the wine was gone, Jesus' mother said to him, "They have no more wine."

4. "Woman, why do you involve me?" Jesus replied. "My hour has not yet come."

5. His mother said to the servants, "Do whatever he tells you."

6. Nearby stood six stone water jars, the kind used by the Jews for ceremonial washing, each holding from twenty to thirty gallons.

7. Jesus said to the servants, "Fill the jars with water"; so they filled them to the brim.

8. Then he told them, "Now draw some out and take it to the master of the banquet."
   They did so,

9. and the master of the banquet tasted the water that had been turned into wine. He did not realize where it had come from, though the servants who had drawn the water knew. Then he called the bridegroom aside

10. and said, "Everyone brings out the choice wine first and then the cheaper wine after the guests have had too much to drink; but you have saved the best till now."

My Lord's Prayer

Our Father, who art in Heaven
Praised & worshipped is Your name
I acknowledge this is no game
And Your will must be done
There are victories waiting to be won
Feed me in the Name of Your Son
See me worthy & pardon my transgressions Lord
As I too forgive those who have trespassed against me
I know the power of unity
So when I face the hills and the valleys
I know that you and that power is around me
As I steadfastly move on through my journey
Thank you for my delivery
Daily you love and cover me
I know You are the Creator
With Power and Dominion over all
I give you all the Glory
Forever and ever
At Your feet I fall.

Amen

"and the master of the banquet tasted the water that had been turned into wine. He did not realize where it had come from, though the servants who had drawn the water knew."

I was 21 when I lost the man who had been the modern day Jesus to me; the one who turned life's water into wine without me even realizing the miraculous things he had done to make sure all was well with me; MY FATHER."

My father died just before I was to graduate from college; he was my primary source of financial stability. He and my mother are the way I made it through college without a student loan. I remember feeling like, why would God take one of the most important pillars in my structure just as I was about to start building another story? I was about to blossom into the rose my parents had groomed and nurtured and watered; but the gardener was gone.

I have so many memories of the time my father took to groom me into the Queen I am today. I remember most of the lessons he taught me as well. I will speak of the ones which have become a part of my intricate design.

My father was a disciplinarian; especially when it came to education. He believed in a militant regime when it came to raising children. He believed in driving fear into us. He believed in corporal punishment and hands on parenting.

He also believed in rewarding people for their accomplishments; he believed in family, community and empowerment.

My father used to beat my ass when he felt he should; he taught me to swim by throwing me in the ocean and telling me my two options; "SINK OR SWIM!"

2

He taught me how to keep my word and not to quit when I declared I wanted to run track. The morning after that declaration, I was awakened at 5 am to go running. He drove alongside me as I ran to the beach where I swam for 30 minutes. He talked to me as he sat in that car; encouraging me and threatening me that now that I have him waking up this early to pursue my goals, "I BETTER NOT QUIT!" He put his foot on the gas and sped ahead of me, telling me I needed to "CATCH UP!"

When I confessed to my father that I was sexually active, we were on a trip in St. Thomas in the US Virgin Islands. I remember we were in traffic when he brought up the boy I was dating; I remember because by the end of this chat I felt I was on a high speed highway playing CHANGING LANES! First he wanted me to know that he liked my boyfriend and that was rare; (my dad liked very few of my friends, especially the boy kind.) Then he pointed out how though we were in separate places, I could still feel that "love" my boyfriend and I shared.

Then he asked me if we were active and I confirmed we were and he asked me what my plans were. I remember responding that I was going to college and "D" would continue his life's pursuits and we would "see where it goes." I remember him asking if it didn't work out; "THEN WHAT?" He also told me that day; "ALLOW NO MAN TO PUT HIS HANDS ON YOU! I AM THE ONLY MAN WHO HAS THE RIGHT TO HIT YOU!" (He so meant that)

He told me that day that if I allowed men to just get what they want from me I won't have much left. He told me I was a prize and that he called me "HIS PRINCESS" because it was meant for me to be raised into a QUEEN. He advised me to choose my KING wisely and to make sure I am always in a position where I am more than just his option; I AM HIS ONLY CHOICE!

He took me to a Gucci store where he had his friend show me an array of beautiful pieces of jewelry and told me to pick what I wanted. I picked out these bamboo earrings and a rope chain. He asked me if I was sure about my choice and I thought about it; especially when he said, "Is that your style?" I realized; they in fact were not MY STYLE; but they were "IN STYLE." He made me confess that as well. He bought my choices for me, but told me not to put them on.

His friend came from a back room with a box and when she opened it; a beautiful set was revealed to me. A matching necklace with pendant; earrings and bracelet set; made of GOLD, DIAMONDS AND SAPPHIRES!

He told me as he put each piece on me right in that store; "LET NO MAN GIVE YOU LESS!"

Love Me Like

Love me like my daddy loved me
So I am reminded of the Queen I am
Like rain drops in a summer storm
Like a lion shielding his family from harm
Love me
Love me like you do in my day dreams
Warm and passionate
Drawing soft erotic screams
Love me like, a millionaire loves his money
Like a bear yearning for his honey
Love me like Rah loved Isis
I'll be your pupil if you will be my iris

Love me fierce
Like our forefathers fought for our freedom
Like you know I'm the one to help you rule your Kingdom
Love me like, a mother does her newborn child
Look into my eyes
Speak into our future with a smile
Like, a father determined to make his son proud
I'll be your beacon if you find yourself lost in the crowd
Love me like a poet loves his pen
Like I'm a part of your brotherhood, let me in
So I can give you more
Show you every side there is to me
Allow you to explore

But first you have to love me

Love me like, I am un-chartered waters
Like you know I am the Most High's daughter
Love me without the trick mirrors
Like it's your destiny to be my hero
Like, a professional boxer loves his hands
Like the All Black Lives matter protesters
Should still be making their demands
Love me like a citizen should understand their rights
Like we know the dream didn't die with Martin
And now is the time to fight
Love me like
Success
Is my middle name
Like my flavor is the same savored
By those who have tasted fame
Love me like, this was meant to be
Like I am unique
Because that's what my daddy told me
Love me.

When the wine was gone, Jesus' mother said to him, "They have no more wine."

My MOTHER has never been one to say, "We have no more wine" she would just squeeze all the grapes we had left; including the sour ones, to make sure our wine continued to flow. She has a way of adding sugar to the water so things always seem sweet.

My mother is a very private person, she hates being in a spotlight and would denounce me if I tell too much of her business (it's the Barbadian Elder in her) She always told me growing up; "keep your business private and you'll never have it told"

So here's what I'll say, my mother was raised by a mother who hooked her donkey to a cart and went out to cane fields to sell lunch to the men and women toiling in the hot sun. She took in the neighborhoods most hopeless youth and by employing them with odd jobs; she inspired a sense of belonging and paying them kept them from robbing her or anyone else.

My mother believes in the same way that souls can be saved if you teach them how live. However, she is a very cautious person and so she loves many but embraces very few. The few she has embraced have tasted the sweetness of her grapes. We have witnessed her stomp juice out of the sour ones and place them in vessels molded out of faith; we heard her pray as they fermented and when it is time to celebrate, Mom knows how to bring in the Spirit.

I am grateful to my mother for many things:

For never seeing a second option

For being a nurturer, especially to my rose; some people will never know how important a relationship between Grandmother and granddaughter is. My child's greatest wealth is her wisdom and it is an inheritance that is handed down through my mother; just as I received mine from hers.

My mother's greatest lesson to me has been not to mix the grapes, grind the sour ones on their own and add whatever was necessary to bring them to my taste. She demonstrates by simply living her life with what is needed to keep her happy. She has shown me you have to take all of the bitter stuff that life has to offer and turn them into sweet wine and most importantly; she taught me what makes the spirit strong.

I'll always love my Mother for these things.

Her

She knew from birth she was to be Mother Earth to a nation
So she prepared herself
Taking in all her elders taught and talked became second nature
For she knew that's where wisdom dwells
Cooking and cleaning is more than a skill, it's a requirement
Learning to do it all develops Self Will, was their encouragement
So she learned

Garnering motherly tendencies along the way by guarding her
siblings while they play
When they were hungry, sleepy or wet
Her needs were always last to be met; it's just the way it is
And when she met her King, she should first meet his
So she's sure that it is really him
They told her, "God will smile through the eyes of his Soul"
So she searched

From books, teachers and loved ones, she collected information
So when it was her time to raise a nation she would be ready
Accepting all the love she could from her daddy
So she knew what it felt like coming from a real man
Like, walking the streets and holding her hand
Pulling her chair and complimenting her hair
Because to him she would always be beautiful
So she wondered

Would he know her?

Would he recognize the diamond under all the coal she had collected?

Because somehow during her upbringing, she had been neglected

See, all that she was prepared for was to help others

The teacher, the nurse, the ref, the chef; the Mother

The one whose compassion would smother her lover

Because she always gives too much

The friend who could heal with just a touch; or a smile

The one who could be trusted to always "Ride or Die"

Though her spirit hungers, she fills others with her words

But who would she be for her?

So she journeyed

Searching high and low for a love like hers would be a catch

To the one who matched; but first she needed to blossom

Become the Rose she was destined to be

Knowing her scent would offend some; but growing was her quest

Feeling her passion pound beneath her chest, begging to be released

But first she had to find her peace

Find the center of her core

For there is where she would find more of herself than she would even know

There is where her river of purpose flowed

The instructions to her rescue

So she studied

Love, shown by example through her Creator above

As a staple; giving it to herself as she would other people

It's nutritional to tender to your own heart

Forgiving herself is where she would start

Then she could do the same to others

The ones who fertilize her roots by forcing her to face the truth

Some trees do bare strange fruits

But that does not decrease her value

So she discovered

That everyone on her path is a part of the Almighty's math

To multiply her portion of His favor

That joy comes from the fruits of her labor

And she should share with her neighbor because her cup; it overflows

She should shine her light wherever she goes

Because even through the darkness she's designed to glow

And amid the pestilence, she is built to grow

Sow, seeds of good intentions will withstand all weapons of destruction

So she pushed

And now, she is HERe

I was in a "relationship" with a man who attracted me with his brilliance! I watched him many times turn water into wine on a business level. His charm and easy going attitude was definitely his key to success. He reminded me so much of my dad, I fell in love. He also taught me a lot. After my father's death, I leaned on this man more than I even noticed and he allowed me.

Months later I was still grieving my father; I was depressed and angry and questioning God about everything. I cried a lot, lost focus on all of my priorities and was simply wilting away.

Then one day one of my close friends who was pregnant and loved for us to do everything together said to me over lunch; "You are pregnant!" I don't remember ever laughing harder than I did that day; right in her face! I told her this was one thing we were NOT going to do together. She insisted on me taking a test and so I obliged because saying no to pregnant women causes STIES!

Imagine my surprise when the THREE tests all agreed with her. ME, Ms. Condom Express…walked with condoms more than I did ID or credit cards. Not because I was promiscuous; but because AIDS was rampant and I was a safe sex rep on my college campus so we distributed condoms regularly. PLUS…I did not have babies in the immediate blueprint I had drawn for myself.

When I told him I was expecting, he allowed me to know he already knew. His words to me were, "I felt you were grieving your father too hard; so I wanted you to have "something" to love!" In my mind I was thinking, "A puppy would have been nice; some fish maybe!"

One year and 10 days after my father's death, my daughter was born and I must say; her father did not just give me "something" to love, I GAVE BIRTH TO MY INSPIRATION!

The most ironic part of this journey was the fact that after planting his seed he has had nothing to do with her being groomed, nurtured nor watered; right before her birth.....the gardener was gone.

Once again, this rose started to wilt! See, my first thought that first day I heard her first cry was;" how am I to navigate this jungle after dropping a petal in the same concrete I had been replanted in?" In addition, "how was I supposed to raise this rose alone; without her gardener; while I was still learning how to grow without MINE?" I looked into her eyes and she answered; PATIENCE AND LOVE!

For 19 years with minimal participation on his part she has grown and blossomed into SOMETHING REMARKABLE and he was right; I LOVE HER WITH MY ALL!

In her I have a double dose of my father; she is Aquarian just like my dad and has that charm and brilliance that attracted me to hers. Her tenacity; well as you read on you'll see where that came from.

Many nights I've cried over her as she slept, praying for God to give me more than my tears to water her dreams. I asked for Him to give me everything I needed to fulfill my job as her mother.

I had an amazing job, a modest home and food. We traveled, made memories and built a bond that can never be broken.

As she grew older and got involved in dance, bowling and doing commercials; our schedules clashed and just as I was about to make a big decision to end some of her activities God sent me a team of angels.

People who we met at these same activities; mothers at her school would pick her up and drop her home or keep her until I picked her up. Sometimes there would be impromptu sleepovers so I could catch my breath. Trusted teenagers would volunteer to baby sit on breaks from school; or take her to bowling or dance.

These are people who are now intricate parts of our village; people who love us and continue to help me to help her grow.

I should have known she would have that kind of support from birth since 7 people paced in a hospital room awaiting her arrival and 14 people stood up in Church as her god-parents. Fourteen supportive individuals dedicated their word to love her and be active in her upbringing; all have kept their word in one way or another.

Others adopted her as their niece or god daughter and their families accepted her as a part of them. As I wished more of my family were in her life; and that her father had not done everything possible to keep her away from his side of her family, God was planting new people in the garden around us. We were being nurtured, groomed and watered. The gardener had returned.

I could have chosen to continue to wilt; could have floated away in the floods of the storm or allowed the changing winds of destruction to pitch me into a gutter of bitterness and despair, I could have but my rose would not allow me to. While I thought my tears were signs of weakness; it was her who told me "Mom, your tears have watered my dreams."

A Rose in Bloom

I was, planted in soil richer than the banks of the Vaal River
Sun-kissed and showered in love
Cool breezes taught me how to dance
I now wave my limbs in praises sent above
I am a rose in bloom

My passage of growth trimmed my waste
Yes, I've been pruned
Sweet fragrance of passion emits during my diffusion
My style is unique but causes no confusion
Yes, I am definitely a rose

Now, some may take a whiff
And turn up their nose
But I keep growing
I'll scatter my seeds, confidently knowing
A new generation is due to come forth

Some look at my pigmentation
And try to determine my worth
But in me is where my value nestles
Lord, I may lose every one of my petals
But please, don't let me lose my roots.

"Woman, why do you involve me?" Jesus replied. "My hour has not yet come."

I remember being 6 months pregnant when he put his hand on my growing stomach and told me "your circle will never be complete." This stemmed from a conversation we were having about my fears that the plans I had for my future would be detoured by me becoming a mother.

I intended to go back to school; get a degree in English and write my way to my destiny. I shared with him my deepest dreams to become a published author with Best Sellers that would write my legacy.

I would have my child at 30 when I would have been over qualified to provide for him or her. By 40, I would have stock piled enough in my bank account that I could stop working and give all my time to help my child navigate through what I consider; the most confusing times of growing up. By 50, they would well be on their way on the stage of adult life and I would be reaping my rewards by watching their success; while celebrating mine.

I spoke of marriage, not necessarily to him because I had already seen signs of his abandonment. I spoke of a love between my King and I that ran deeper than a willow tree's roots; stronger than her trunk and wider than her branches. One that stood out above the others in this jungle we call life. It would blossom beautiful fragrances and bare amazing off-spring that would not grow too far from the tree. It would drink the waters and dance with the winds of the storms; all negativity and adversity would serve as fertilizer.

I knew I deserved a love that would always grow and could offer shelter for me as well as others; one I could nestle in and feel safe. A love that would not stunt our individual growth, but instead; it would allow us to securely branch out and do things that would reinforce our roots. I am destined to have a love that weathers all seasons and lives on through generations.

I spoke of children raised by both parents into Kings and Queens; including the one I carried. I even told him I knew him and I wouldn't survive, but I trusted that the child we created would reap the benefits of having us separately in their life.

He responded; "your circle will never be complete."

When I asked what that meant; he said, "that plan for the life you want will never reach full circle; you'll always be missing a piece."

It was the day I had to chase him on foot at 8 months along; that I recognize what he meant in regards to our daughter. He jumped a turnstile to get away from a woman who could barely see her own feet. Then a few days after she was born he had 3 cases of milk delivered from a store with a note on the receipt saying; "congratulations on the birth of your daughter." "YOUR!" That was probably the most he's contributed to her having a full meal.

I accepted that he had abandoned her and vowed that would not deter me from my plans for us. It was just going to be a different road taken; one of a single mother. Just as I came to that painful realization I met and married within six months; my Romeo.

He was a smooth operator who used his simple, yet sophisticated demeanor and handsome, rugged charm to woo me, my child and my entire family into his web of deception.

It was a whirl wind romance that included weekly date nights, even after marriage. We had many family dinners and parties with both sides of the family in attendance. His family welcomed my child and I with Judas arms; but at that time it felt like we were welcomed. He would randomly surprise me with gifts of jewelry, clothes he picked out himself and shoes he thought would be beautiful on my feet; and roses. Every Friday, I received roses. He asked my mom first; then I said "Yes!" He moved in; we got married.

My friends became his, yet I knew only a fistful of his. They were the ones he "trusted around his family." We visited their homes and they visited ours. We double dated, went to church together and shared many laughs. He showed me such love, I felt like my dreams were coming together.

He also showed great interest in my writing and in my job and my finances. He would pop up on my job and chat cheerfully with my co-workers; then later warn me about letting certain ones get too close. Friends of the family that seemed to close to me warranted the same warning. If I met someone new, he would ask if they knew about him.

He felt it was best if we kept our finances in one place, so I put my money in his bank account. I would write out the checks to our creditors and landlord and give him to sign and mail. I saw the same amounts deducted from the account so I knew the bills were paid. He was so fiscally responsible; that's why I never questioned his new music, designer colognes, sneakers and outfits or expensive jewelry. Besides, he worked at a law office and made just a little less than me; but I was sure we could afford it.

We made it to our first year; still deep in bliss. Celebrated our first anniversary at our favorite restaurant where our usual waiter refused to serve us. She must have had a hard day I thought; it was weird the way she behaved, but we still had an amazing night. I was even surprised the next day when I discovered I did not get sick from the food like I usually would.

I started to discover other things soon after that; like, his co-worker who would talk my ears off on the phone when I called. She started to quickly rush off our calls; and the baby sitter quit. There was that girlfriend of mine whose husband he thought might be into me; she slowly pulled away from our friendship. His daughter's mother; who at first wanted me to have nothing to do with her child; she was calling and telling me all the kid lacked and I would buy these things so he could take them to her.

Then he started getting drunk; in the beginning he could barely handle one beer. Our love making went from soft and sweet, to erotic and freaky and then violating.

Love taps turned to pushes, pushes to shoves; shoves to slaps, kicks, chokes and punches.

The lies started to spring up, there were also those nights "his baby" did not want him to leave so he stayed until she fell asleep; leading to him missing the last ferry and having to spend the night. Or, her mother needed a baby sitter so she could go to work and he wanted to spend time with his daughter so he volunteered; but she worked a double and he had to go to work the next day from her home.

There was also the baby sitter he grew up with and could trust her because they were close. She quit and called several months later demanding child support.

The reason I did not get sick the night of our anniversary was because our "favorite waitress" did not serve us. Seems she did not expect me at that celebration. Let me not forget "Peaches" the stripper.

The co-worker did not want to talk to me as much because she feared her tongue would release the fact that a girl in the mail room had just been fired for approaching the Paralegal in their department and telling her that she was pregnant for her boyfriend. The paralegal then responded, "That is his wife's problem."

Then there was the Fiancée; they met over the phone and convinced each other they were the perfect match. So for 5 months he traveled back and forth to another state on "job and music related business" Then he came home and told me he wanted to try this next state out; the job would relocate him and we could come later. He would need money for the move, so he opened a second account he could transfer funds to and from.

He called me every day, but the number I had for him was giving problems so at night he was unreachable. Then the letter I sent to tell him about my miscarriage of the baby we conceived the night before he left; returned to sender.

The checks I wrote to cover our rent were being returned as well; and my landlord only wanted cash. Lights were cut, so was the gas and before I could catch myself; eviction.

He was gone! So was my money, dignity, home and self-esteem.

I lived through this; and when he left he took my last hope. Any chance that I had of becoming a legal resident rested with him. We were submitting documents to immigration through an attorney on his job. I had not even received a receipt for the ones we had already sent. I anticipated an appointment; but the system was backed up and so it was taking a long time. It never came.

I eventually regained composure of my life; my village came to my rescue and helped me to stand again. I still had my job and now I was writing poetry people were coming to pay at the door to hear. They were even buying copies of my pieces for a dollar each.

I had found us a beautiful home and it was close to school and the park. Baby girl and I were back full throttle; taking trips and going to Knicks games, eating at high end restaurants; and then he found us.

Back to the old, sweet romantic "him" filled with promises that included my freedom.

We "dated" for another 6 months trying to work things out, he slept over but I somehow could not get aroused by him so sex was not a part of the equation.

He claimed to understand until he found out I had a male friend who I spoke to frequently. Someone who had been there for me in my many times of need; but we were just friends. He sat listening to a conversation one night; I did as I always did at the end of a chat with someone close. I told my friend I loved him.

He came out to the living room that night and started an argument; according to him it was because I was with another man that I could not fulfill my "wifely duties." I told him it was not that; but because the last time we were sexual, was the first and only time I had contracted an STD. I had no medical insurance and had to pay to clear that up; so I was definitely not into taking neither the physical nor financial risk.

I had bruised his ego without trying; I was being honest. He went back to the room and I made my bed on the couch and dozed off. I was awakened to find him on top of me grunting his way to ecstasy and everything in me died that night.

I went to work the next day like nothing happened, when I returned home; everything of his was gone and it was like he was never there. Except he left the fragrance of his cologne all over my home, on my pillows and sheets; and in the bathroom is where I found the bottle. I thought, "Maybe this was the new way for dogs to leave their scent."

This rose started to wilt again, but this time I couldn't just move on. I had to prune myself; start new. I chopped my hair off and twisted them into locks; new growth was my goal and I decided to start with my roots.

I remember like it was yesterday; my friend and her family brought my Angel home after she spent the weekend with them and she cried her eyes out, begging me to go get my hair back.

What a mess I had made; what an even bigger mess I had become. I stayed my focus on my job and keeping my child happy. I felt I had to over compensate for what was missing in her life, so we got involved in so many social activities I sometimes got our schedules confused.

Many saw me as irresponsible when they would see me out late at night with her. None knew that being at home brought back the monsters in my head and I needed to be away from there as much as possible. So, I would wear her out and come home. I would put her to bed and after taking care of my motherly duties; I would grab my book, pen and a bottle. They had become my coping mechanisms and eventually; my vices.

It started with wine, and eventually led to vodka. I kept the same job through it all (another vice), moving further and further up the leadership ladder. I started dedicating more time and energy, learning new skills and taking on new responsibilities; all to ensure I kept that job. It was all I had to keep my baby safe and to keep me distracted from my reality. I knew it wasn't meant for me to go through that mess for too long.

I was still writing…..and telling myself "My hour has not yet come."

Living on a Prayer

She came to the land of opportunity with a dream
Her vision was clairvoyant, but she did not hear the screams
Deafened by a naïve mentality
That she had reached the land of liberty
One nation under God
She was greatly impressed by media's façade
Of that 40 acres and a mule
She believed she could make it on her God given tools
Her talents, her brain and her heart
She fought for good grades so her plan had a jump start
By 21, she was a woman with a degree
A great job and a nice life filled with glee
And then one day; she met.....he.

He who treated her like a Queen
Who meant what he said and said nothing he would mean
But he was that piece to her puzzle
Young and distinguished and he loved to cuddle
Candles and dinners both crafted by his hand
An education, great job, happy life and a real man
How did her life get like this?

She whispered many prayers and made many a wish
But somehow, her needs got lost in translation
Because from the news of gestation
His affection started to come from his fist

She kept looking around for who controlled that switch
And each time she would come away with a black eye
No one sees her scars, none hears her cries
Make up and a smile, she wears as her disguise
But inside, she's locked in a prison
She must obey the rules and execute them with precision
If she and her baby were to survive
She took every hit and counted the days of their lives
When love lived there

There was no objection to their union
And she was convinced he'd been changed as they shared their first communion
She mentally documented his first smile
As he looked down with love, into the eyes of their child
And made promises, he promised he would keep
He swore happiness would be her only reason to weep
How did her life get like this?

He had validated her position by changing her name from miss
And then he tried to delete her
With the same arms he held her, he mercilessly beat her
And then whispers, "you are the cause of all this"
After he rolls off her battered body, he gives a sweet kiss
As if that would erase the shame
Her body became his after she took his last name
He told her patience was the key to her liberation
She would one day enjoy freedom through immigration
She would finally taste how it felt to win

And when it was all said and done she'll owe it all to him

Till then, loving him was her only liberty

So she lives on a prayer, a prayer that one day she'll be free.

"Nearby stood six stone water jars, the kind used by the Jews for ceremonial washing, each holding from twenty to thirty gallons."

I learned during this part of the journey that "delay is not denial."

When I least expected it, LOVE walked into my life. It was what I now refer to as my "NEW GROWTH LOVE."

We were like two ships coming out of dark, stormy waters. The same waters, just different directions; shipwrecked from the turbulence; we found each other.

It was the bright light in my daughter's eyes that guided us to the same shores. She knew him way before I had even met him and had formed this amazing "kinship" with him. After a very awkward encounter involving her running away from me in the street and jumping in his arms gleefully screaming his name; we were introduced by the very happy 5 year old and later by the adult responsible for them meeting each other.

We became cool friends; discovering we had a number of things in common and we each had other interests that the next didn't mind exploring.

He was refreshing and exciting; exactly what I needed in my life! I think what was really intriguing to me was the fact that I was not looking for; neither was I interested in a relationship at that time. Yet here was this man fulfilling most of the voids in my life at that time.

We were friends for an entire year; talking and sharing our stories with each other.

It seemed we were living polar lifestyles. He was in pain because he truly wanted to be a father to his children; but he was caught in the barb wire fence of child support that allowed him only one day in the weekend to physically be a father; at the cost of $1200.00 per month.

I was desperate for my daughter's father to stand up and be a man and father to his child; I didn't even want his money!

I remember us one night sitting in a bar drinking vodka like it was water. He had just hung up from a conversation with the woman who had custodial rights over his children and her boyfriend. They told him it was up the "boyfriend" if he would be able to see his children on the weekends any longer.

According to the happy couple, they were working on being a family and that required him getting to know the children. So, he lost his weekend privileges. I was just a great drinking buddy; so I drank with him and tried to talk him out of "taking a ride." I have stamped in my mind the moment I saw his tears fall into that glass of vodka.

Now, he was also a very popular person and I recognized early that women fell just from his smile. So, I made the decision that we would just be friends; he however, had decided that he would have me.

He made me happy; mostly because my daughter was besotted by him. She intoxicated me with the love and joy she felt for him.

The love between them was so obvious that it made it easy for my village to embrace him when we finally decided to date.

I thought it was ironic that while we were just friends no one interfered with our friendship; I had met his family, his children and friends; co-workers and even his church family.

Shortly after we became an item, the past relationships popped up. People we met together started doing strange things. Females I called friends repeatedly; disrespectfully tried their luck. They were all ages too; even in the church. I remember this one sister in the church who kept asking me; "Why he loves you so?" At first; I thought she meant God because he was delivering me through all kinds of turbulence in my spiritual life. Later, I found out she meant my "NGL" (New Growth Love)

We celebrated a challenged love for quite a few years. I say celebrate because all sorts of issues beyond the females came into play. Together we fought hard and strong, and together we won. He was my loudest fan as I stood on stages and spit poetic vows to him; testified about his exotic love through prose and took rooms full of people on journeys. He truly supported my grind, even though he was not at all into poetry.

He enjoyed the light and even reached for it by getting back into a lost passion; singing.

He brought me back to the church; first as a guest performer for a fundraiser they were hosting. Then I voluntarily walked to the front of that church and re-accepted Christ as my Lord God and personal savior.

I remember that Sunday morning vividly; the sermon was from John 4; the WOMAN AT THE WELL. I sat there and listened to the minister break down how Jesus sat at the well and asked her for a drink of water. She was amazed that he was speaking to her; they were not the same kind and she a Samaritan; was beneath a Jew.

"10 Jesus answered and said unto her, If thou knewest the gift of God, and who it is that saith to thee, Give me to drink; thou wouldest have asked of him, and he would have given thee living water.

11 The woman saith unto him, Sir, thou hast nothing to draw with, and the well is deep: from whence then hast thou that living water?

12 Art thou greater than our father Jacob, which gave us the well, and drank thereof himself, and his children, and his cattle?

13 Jesus answered and said unto her, Whosoever drinketh of this water shall thirst again:

14 But whosoever drinketh of the water that I shall give him shall never thirst; but the water that I shall give him shall be in him a well of water springing up into everlasting life.

15 The woman saith unto him, Sir, give me this water, that I thirst not, neither come hither to draw.

16 Jesus saith unto her, Go, call thy husband, and come hither.

17 The woman answered and said; I have no husband. Jesus said unto her, Thou hast well said, I have no husband:

18 For thou hast had five husbands; and he whom thou now hast is not thy husband: in that saidst thou truly."

She was stained by her past; condemned by her present and cursed for her origin. She admitted her life and her indiscretions to Jesus. As have I.

"21 Jesus saith unto her, Woman, believe me, the hour cometh, when ye shall neither in this mountain, nor yet at Jerusalem, worship the Father.

22 Ye worship ye know not what: we know what we worship: for salvation is of the Jews.

23 But the hour cometh, and now is, when the true worshippers shall worship the Father in spirit and in truth: for the Father seeketh such to worship him.

24 God is a Spirit: and they that worship him must worship him in spirit and in truth.

25 The woman saith unto him, I know that Messias cometh, which is called Christ: when he is come, he will tell us all things.

26 Jesus saith unto her, I that speak unto thee am he."

Yet, He spoke to her. I was worthy enough to hear him; I had to believe that.

"27 And upon this came his disciples, and marvelled that he talked with the woman: yet no man said, What seekest thou? or, Why talkest thou with her?

28 The woman then left her waterpot, and went her way into the city, and saith to the men,

29 Come, see a man, which told me all things that ever I did: is not this the Christ?

30 Then they went out of the city, and came unto him.

31 In the mean while his disciples prayed him, saying, Master, eat.

32 But he said unto them, I have meat to eat that ye know not of.

33 Therefore said the disciples one to another, Hath any man brought him ought to eat?

34 Jesus saith unto them, My meat is to do the will of him that sent me, and to finish his work."

I discovered I had a purpose. That; after I had searched through a variation of religions to find him, he was right there just waiting for me to have a chat.

"behold, I say unto you, Lift up your eyes, and look on the fields; for they are white already to harvest.

36 And he that reapeth receiveth wages, and gathereth fruit unto life eternal: that both he that soweth and he that reapeth may rejoice together.

37 And herein is that saying true, One soweth, and another reapeth."

This activated my mission. I would sow and even though "My hour has not yet come;" it was ok for others to reap.

Come meet a Man

Come meet a man
Who has made promises I know that he will keep
A man who looked into my soul, deep
Saw my wounds and healed me
A man who will not deceive me
He loves me from my hair follicles
To my toe nails
Told me if I trust in Him
I would never fail
Come meet this man.

Come meet a man
Who met me when I was down
I had nothing and no one
My smile was really a frown
Come meet this man who
Loves me for me
Has opened my eyes
And allowed me to see
LIFE!

Not just any life
But a life of my own
A life where there is progress
And I can see my growth
A life where He is my guidance

My protector, my friend
A life that when it' over
I'll look forward to the end
Come meet this man.

*Inspired by the story of the Woman at the Well

We were a vital part of each other's maturation to the next stage in life. We also had an addiction for each other; one that would last way past the expiration date of our relationship.

See, I exercised my new purpose with him quite generously. I sowed seeds and allowed him to reap the harvest. There were times there was hardly anything to reap; but I gave, he took and I survived off the remains.

I was fine with this because that made me feel wanted. I needed that kind of love, it made me feel irreplaceable.

And for a while I was too; then things started to change and after I had been:

- The only accomplice in his escape from the grips of child support
- His shoulder to cry on
- The executor of his game plan to defeat the battles we faced
- His cheat sheet
- The reinforcement in his foundation
- The cement for a house I never got to even move in to

We became two ships coming out of dark, stormy waters. The same waters, just different directions; shipwrecked from the turbulence; we lost each other in the fog.

I lost a great love, and sacrificed a lot; but in that pain I discovered a deeper love for myself and even though I thought I would have been married to him I now know that he was just a part of the journey. He is a better man today; and deserves a woman strong enough to stand with him, for him; and UP TO him.

He still has a kinship with my guiding light; that bond was damaged in the storms but not beyond repair.

I walked away from this field with nothing but sour grapes; I was shattered by this devastation and found myself on a mountain with God whispering in my ear **"Your hour has not yet come."**

Capsized

I sat back last night
And discovered that you and I had lost our love
I cried as I acknowledged that this journey is now over
It's over
I look into your eyes
And I don't even recognize you
You laid me across a blanket made of deception
I reached my arms up
And asked God, could this get any worse
You entered my heart first
And made your way to my cerebral
Where, a battle between my head and heart erupted
You left my spirit feeling soiled and corrupted
You, robbed my soul of her song
And tried to silence her poetry
You took my trust and built on it
A pyramid of love affairs
Weaved into a blueprint
Of what we once called love
Slowly, I came to a realization
I was no longer floating on clouds of euphoria
Instead; my day dreams are now nightmares
The foundation we dug together
Has a crack like the liberty bell
It can't be repaired
You have broken my heart

And my pain
Through my pen
Flows freely
You took all that you could take from me
And then headed for more.

I sat back last night
And discovered that you and I had lost our love
I cried
As I acknowledged that this journey is now over
It's over
I looked into your eyes
And accepted that you really don't love me
You laid me across
What felt like a bed of hot coal
I reached my arms up
And asked myself if I didn't deserve more
You ran circles around me
Gave me just enough of your loving
To satisfy the craving that rumbled inside of me
Abusing my offering
And enforcing that I loved you more than I love myself
You, move with the tendencies of a ravenous predator
I swore
I knew exactly what love felt like
And then you slaughtered..... my...... soul
I landed in a pool of confusion

Struggling to breathe
As you, selfishly walked away
The pain you caused burned like the lava from a volcano
I found myself lost in transition
Our love became a tornado
The explosions went off
And I saw
Faded dreams
And flashbacks
Of what this was meant to be
Finally resurrected
I activated the new me

I sat back last night
And discovered that you and I had lost our love
I cried as I acknowledged that this journey is now over
It's over ....It's over........It's over

If you reference back through this book you'll find many references of; "planting bad seeds, broken or empty vessels, sour grapes, scarce harvest."

Up to this hour, I am grateful to God for the next love he sent my way.

Through all that you've read so far in this part of the journey, my AWAKENING LOVE was an intricate part of my life. He was my escape; the one I ran to whenever things fell apart. He was my advisor, my booster.

He loved me in my rawest and my rarest forms and I knew he loved me. He made me smile at the hardest times; and he made me sing Karaoke. We danced together to no music, laughed at each other's craziness and would always be there whenever the next called. We listened to gospel at 5 am and rocked out to house music anytime we felt like it.

He called me fabulous and introduced me as Queen. I knew he meant those things because he had always treated me in that manner. When we spent time together, it was just us. Uninterrupted hours of his attention; compliments and the most brutally honest conversations I've ever had. He pointed out my flaws and highlighted my "fabulousity" at times he even bragged about me.

He made me feel the closest to the way my daddy loved me. We had many unfinished talks about us coming together over the years.

I can be honest with myself now and admit; I never felt I brought enough to the table for him. I was planting bad seeds and allowing others to turn me into a broken or empty vessel. I was grinding sour grapes and was forced to drink the wine alone. I reaped scarce harvest and at some point accepted myself as barren land.

He knew my fight and saw my tenacity; held me while I cried out my defeat and allowed me to lick my wounds. He picked me up many times over the years. He knew my potential; and he had proven his.

We got together; and at first it was so surreal. Who would have thought that after him knowing all of my flaws and most of my weaknesses and lacks; he would still want me to be his Queen.

I was sure this was it; we had both gone through the highs and lows of relationships, shared chapters in each other's lives. He knew things only few others knew and he had always been protective of me and my character.

And then all of that changed; there were people and incidents that were able to find cracks and made it their mission to prove me as just refurbished. Somehow, despite all he and I had built together; they won and not only did I lose my greatest love, I lost one of my most cherished friends. I still cannot explain the void I feel when I think of him that pain of losing someone I valued so deeply and to see the efforts taken to destroy what really was a beautiful kind of love has been unbearable sometimes.

During this experience I discovered an even deeper love for myself; I found something that I kept giving away throughout each of the relationships I write about. I still love him and always will; but despite how I feel, he too; is a part of the journey. I have also accepted that; "My hour has not yet come."

The four vessels of love I speak about may not seem to have been much about love; I know.

It took another vessel to point out the one thing each of them had in common. They are all good people to other people. Every last one of them were; or are still involved in the uplifting and advance of community.

The latter two are committed family men; especially to their mothers. Essentially they all loved me at first; but then I fell off because instead of maintaining the one thing that drew them in; I relinquished it and eventually lost it to their egos; I gave them my POWER; in exchange for their LOVE.

I Yearn

I yearn to live a simple life where love penetrates my deepest
sorrows

And laughter heals my wounds

To live like tomorrow is today

And rainbows decorate my world so I know when the storms are
over

I yearn to love the one who sees my darkest fears

And lights fire that blaze the way straight to his arms

To listen to his heart beat rhythms interrupted only by murmurs
of how much he loves me back

I yearn to continue to learn how to be a better me than the day
before

And turn soil infused with faith to nurture

To sow seeds with roots reaching back to times when we were
Kings and Queens

Singing praise as I await the harvest

I yearn to reign in my Queendom

With principles set by my ancestral mothers

When crowns adorned their heads and knowledge made them a
dime

To raise young royals who live to an age that's prime

I yearn

I yearn to sing freedom songs with stanzas sweet like honey on
my throat

And lyrics that break chains

To dance like a ballerina with the heart of a djembe drummer
invoking the spirits of our fore-fathers

I yearn to fight

Not to stand equal to another

But unified with my sisters and brothers to be outstanding

To build bridges that reconnect generations and create stories that
are ours

My yearnings stem from years of lack of the simple

Fears of tomorrow and nightmares of yesterday

From lending my heart to thieves who stole what I gave freely
while taking my freedom away

From losing hope in the greatness within me

And forgetting lessons of my ancestry

Allowing myself to be trapped in slavery, neglectful of my
birthright; royalty

From silencing my voice and dancing to others' beat

While standing in the cold and still taking the heat

It comes from pain

From standing in the rain

From a lack of faith in God and His favor; which for me is
ordained

I failed to love me

Neglected to examine myself truthfully

So now I yearn

I learn to live, love and laugh

I yearn to breathe

"Fill the jars with water"; so they filled them to the brim.

I was left broken and empty in the first 2 relationships mentioned here; after the latter two, I was left hurt.

By recognizing the difference in the effects each relationship had on me, they now stand as empty jars because I have taken back my life.
I could have let those effects consume me, but I know now that they were just another part of the journey.

Some people will come into your life to empty your already empty soul and steal what's left of your spirit. Others will come into your life and replenish you. What has helped me to continue pass my empty times is my village.

"My Village; a collective of blood relatives, strangers, loved ones and invested ones who stand as vessels filled with love at a depth that runs roots deep."

When I sit back and think about the way God had intricately woven our lives together into a patchwork of love; I am humbled.

Until I was already a mother and things started to fall apart, I was blind to my blessings. It was late into my pregnancy and the gardener was already gone. My phone rang and woke me from my sleep; wrong number.

That incident repeated multiple times over the following 4 weeks before the caller engaged me in a conversation that lasted well into the night. My voice that night was labored because it felt like my "Inspiration" was standing up in my stomach after she demanded an entire pizza for dinner.

He asked me if I was okay and I described how I felt exactly that way. Then I burst into tears and shared my life with a total stranger over the phone. He listened intently and then; as if he knew me, he told me that it was meant for me to take this journey and if there was any way he could help; please let him.

We met face to face several weeks after that and from the day she was born until now; he has stood by my side as my friend and dedicated godfather to my "Inspiration."

Her godmother traveled from overseas to stand by me; and for her at her christening. Spoiling her ridiculously with fashions way beyond her needs; but I had no choice but to indulge her.

She has indulged me in crying my eyes out; using her as a sounding board for my plans, pulling me back up if I faltered. She has scolded me and hugged me at the same time. She knows my mind so well that certain words trigger signals in her, letting her know I am in distress without me saying it. She knows my language and she's been this way since our childhood. She calls me the "Comeback Kid;" I call her, Motivation.

At three months old her uncle held her in his arms for the first time. He looked her in the eyes and told her she would never be treated like a baby. He promised to be there for her at all times.

He has been a pillar in our lives. He is a Chief in our village; his wisdom and love is a beacon to any who may be lost. I call him my little brother, but the truth is he is a "Giant" in my life.

His strength and determination is iron in the blood that pumps through the veins of our tribe. He is another sounding board for me and my harshest critic. We've had unbelievable fights and disagreements; and we will fight an unbelievable fight for each other.

He picks my ideas down to crumbs and then helps me remold them into delicacies. He challenges my spirituality and my commitment; and then uses the Word to show me instances where I am repeating the past. He will always hold the key to one of the biggest chambers in my heart. He is my "Spirit's Guide"

Authentic as I've never known is the next vessel. Having her in my life has given me the chance to relive a lot of my mistakes and intervene before she does the same. She is my purest relationship.

"Tested and tried

Took hits but the love never dies

When trust is the rock on which it's built"

She is that one person I know for sure, anything she's said about me has been said to me; first. She is brutally real; honest, sarcastic and abrasive. There is no sugar coating with her; yet she is who I go to if I need my soul, senses or feelings scrubbed!

First, she exfoliates then she replenishes. She is the perfect everything she is to me and as I type I know she's going to make me eat all of the nice things I've written on this page.

The truth is my Sister, you have refilled me the most and plugged more holes in my life. You add to my life in ways I know only God could have provided and I am grateful to have you as my Clarity.

When I think of this sister, Nzinga comes to mind. We met in college as I was navigating through a new educational system and in the process of finding myself.

Through doing the work of the Black Student Union we bonded; building a sisterhood while fighting for student rights and uplifting the student body as a whole.

She showed me every trick there was to make it through college without falling prey to the distractions there. She taught me how to align myself with the right folks in the student body and faculty. She kept me under her wing and so when it was time for her to graduate she held an election and before I blinked twice, I was the newly elected president of the B.S.U.

This was an opportunity to meet new people; famous ones too! Along with the Student Government President; I met Rev. Jesse Jackson and Al Sharpton when we held a rally on their behalf on campus. I was thrown on my first stage of public speaking that day as I had to do an introduction of the Rev. Jackson. I was also responsible for bringing Wendy Williams to campus to discuss Breast Cancer Awareness.

I learned to work hard; study hard and fight hard. She was a single mother who worked and studied to make things better for her family. Her King had been taken by violence way to early and she vowed to honor him in raising their daughter; their Queen.

I remember the sisters in the B.S.U taking turns on our breaks to watch Queen so Nzinga could go to class. We did that for all the moms and dads in our club. It was part of building our village. I learned to ask the right questions and assert myself; but most importantly, I learned how to be a good sister. I learned what SISTERHOOD truly means.

Today she is still my Nzinga; still fighting and winning battles to protect her beautiful "Queen."

Love is the flag flown high from the heart of this next vessel. She makes me want to fight her; those who constantly hurt her and with her to make sure she reaches her goals.

Her faith is resilient and she means well. She inspires the activist in me because she is always on the battle field. If I had to make a biblical connection to our relationship I would have to say we are Esther and Ruth.

I have a Dream Whisperer; she listens to my dreams and speaks words of fruition into them. She calmly checks me as I rant or panic about issues and then she gives me food from the Word to replace all my wasted energy.

She is a survivor in every sense of the word and she continually teaches me how to Celebrate Life.

Joy, I call her my Joy because it does not matter what I'm going through she finds a way to bring Joy and light to any situation. She walks with me as though she was assigned to me, Divinely. She taught me how to look past situations and find resolve. She is warm and loving even while giving the tongue lashing of a lifetime.

She is with me through my elevation from stage to stage.

If anyone had told me that performing for a small conference in NYC would lead to the next vessel's influence on my life; I would not have believed them. I performed with a group and after the event she approached me and said, "Next year I am hosting a Women's Empowerment Conference and I need you to perform."

At first I thought she wanted the entire group but she specified; "YOU!"

I was promoting my published book of poetry, "Impressions of a Poet; Footnotes of my Journey." She bought copies in bulk and raffled them during her event; helping my promotion. My performance led to additional sales and bookings to appear as a feature in other events.

She taught me how to take my passion and turn it into profit and one year later when I returned to share the stage with my daughter and 3 of her friends doing dance interpretation to my poetry; I found my purpose.

This next vessel came into my life during a tumultuous time of my journey and she has been a strong tower of resilience. She has taught me that it pays to be authentic and genuine and to believe in the power of the Universe.

She helped me to see that it does not matter what personal issues one might be enduring; if the opportunity comes along to help someone else and you can, then you should. She loves with the freedom of a bird in flight and is very protective of those she loves.

I want to tell about all of the vessels in my life that have poured into me and filled me to the brim; but that's another book. I would be remiss to not mention my brother from another mother who has helped me to be a better mother by allowing me to be a part of his journey as a single father. His defiant fight to keep his daughter as a constant part of his life has taught me how to keep pushing for what I know is mine. Fathers often get the bad rap when the relationship falls apart. I can truly say the fathers I know work hard to be prominent in the lives of their children. His daughter is my "Sunshine"

Other vessels I must mention include the sister that allowed me her couch to call my own and her kids love me like I was always a part of their family. Also, the brother who reminded me that; "Faith without works is death."

"and the master of the banquet tasted the water that had been turned into wine. He did not realize where it had come from, though the servants who had drawn the water knew. "

"Not everyone takes the time to really savor your true flavor. They sample and appreciate only that which teases their taste buds. Some will take the time to really figure out if you are for their palate; others will consume you out of greed.

I'm learning that if I keep living in fear of the unknown; I'll be living in vain! I'M COMING OUT FROM BENEATH THESE CLOUDS!!!!" Empress Poetry© 8/4/15

This was the hardest part to write because I had to face all of my fears in efforts to complete this book. I feared facing the champion whom I allowed to be defeated by giving her power to others.

I dreaded facing the fact that in essence; I had betrayed myself. I had to admit that they were times I felt like a hypocrite; I was empowering others to fight as I was simultaneously giving up.

The day you have to face yourself and admit your wrongs to her or him. That; will be the most torrential day of your life. The emotional wave you will ride will either guide you to the shores or you'll experience a wipeout.

I often thought about writing my story and then I would toss the idea right out of my head; but like my sister always say; "Some of this stuff you just can't make up!" So I have to tell MY TRUTHS. I say that because I've come to realize that some folks see this as me telling their business; when in fact I'm telling my story.

At some point I guess they will see how what they consider their business was simply just another chapter in my life; they are just another part of my journey.

I've often been told that I always make things about me. That use to bother me because I have never been a selfish person. Then I had to acknowledge the status of that statement. I always heard that whenever I had to defend myself against unfair or deliberate attacks against my character. Or, when I am addressing issues that affect me and the individual I am dealing with is in defense mode.

I've been in situations where I admit to people that "I need help" and they hear "I need sympathy" I wondered why and discovered it was because some people see you go through stuff and come out a winner and think all is well. They fail to see the internal damage; the spiritual devastation and the mental strain.

I've been in some winning situations and came out the loser. I've had my dreams snatched by demons because they saw my vision and my possibilities.

I've been beaten and robbed; of money and opportunities.

I've been employed by some amazing people who saw my potential and invested in my development and growth. I've worked for others who took total advantage of my dedication and commitment. I've worked for Jews and Italians that paid me my worth and Jamaicans and Guyanese who made me question my worth.

I had a boss who knew I was desperate for work and that I was undocumented and made a job I loved a total nightmare. Shorten wages and humiliation; sexual harassment and accusations. I remember him smacking my butt as I stood by a file cabinet and when I protested he commented that everything in that office was his.

When I stood my ground about not working on Sundays because I attended church every Sunday with my daughter; he responded that God is not a fool, he knows that I need a job to support my family and pay tithes so my job was more important than God and my family.

He also stuck his hand down my shirt one day; for feels.

I ran the front office of an Immigration law Firm for $7.00/hr; got promoted to Paralegal for $7.50/hr and though I felt totally oppressed by the sister I worked for; it was the most rewarding job of my life.

There I was; an undocumented immigrant helping others get their piece of freedom. To some that might have been torture; to me it was a rehearsal. Every time a client got approved, I celebrated with them and imagined the joy I would feel the day I got approved.

Every denial was a chance to review for vital mistakes or inaccuracies. With 30 days to respond it meant there was no time to mourn the first denial; we had to get that file right. Then we practiced seed, time, harvest; we had planted the seed by reviewing, correcting and re-filing within the allowed time, now we pray during the time it took for INS to make a decision. I will always hold dear the many thanks and compliments I received for simply doing my job. The days I made calls to notify clients of the final decision in their favor; HARVEST! I took a lot of life lessons from those experiences; I learned *DELAY IS NOT ALWAYS DENIAL.*

I was also able to use my gift of poetry to uplift clients that were incarcerated and fighting deportation. There was one lady that called weekly just so we could talk about her case; but she also needed my words and I spent many hours talking to her. She may never know how she helped me; listening to her speak about her children being without her and feeling trapped; having given up her freedom to gain nothing. It made me appreciate the fact that daily my daughter's tiny fingers caressed my face as she kissed me and told me she loves me. Though living with many lacks, I was still free enough to live my life and be there for my child.

Another young lady was working on her fiancée visa to come here and marry the love of her life. He had such a passion to be with her that I worked over time to get their documents done. I attended that wedding and was asked to be their daughter's god-mother. Her first child; who was 9 at the time of her approval just entered Howard University as a freshman.

That job taught me compassion and patience. I endured the borderline abuse of my boss because there was a sweet taste of hope in each approval I was a part of.

Someone said writing is therapeutic and another declared "Reading is fundamental;" as I continue to write this book this process has proven both to be true.

It is not easy reliving a journey like mine, mostly because you tend to remember people who have been a part of molding you; who are no longer here. I've lost very few close people; but those that I have lost were monumental to me.

I've already mentioned the impact of my father's death; no need to revisit that. My grandmother was my next hit and I tried to pull it together and be there for my mother as much as I could but my "Mamie"; she introduced me to my soul.

I would hear her talking alone all the time; in my naivety I thought she was just getting old. One day I asked her why she talked to herself and she laughed a hearty laugh and started singing the song "No never alone."

Her laugh was intoxicating and I learned that her cutest laugh came whenever she acknowledged God had stepped in and fixed things. She helped people a lot and her theme song was "Love is a flag flown high from the castle of my heart;" she lived that.

She encouraged me to forgive myself for having a baby out of wedlock and empowered me to do all I can for my daughter even if her father wasn't there. I still have the final letter she wrote me and remember the last line said; "take care of Pumpkin and go back to God."

My favorite homosexual cousin and guardian who taught me how to cook, wash, clean; not as a child but as a woman. He taught me the correct way to put a condom on using a banana as our model and told me everything; down to the freakiest about sex.

He introduced me to a grass skirt and dance at 3 years old; and Anita Baker. Fashion and makeup tips; even though I was not allowed to wear makeup and he fought like a warrior on my behalf. I remember him standing on the hill and telling a young woman who attempted to bully my brother and I; just how he would slap, murder and dispose of her if she ever uttered another word to or about us.

I love and miss him sorely; but I always know when his spirit is near.

When I first moved here I spent most of my free time between my cousin and a childhood friend who is another of my daughter's godmothers. Whenever we spent time together we had a blast. She took me bowling for the first time and air shot the ball down the lane like her name was Jordan. The lady on the lane next to us must have been a serious bowler because she was mad at us. She started to scold us on the proper way to bowl when my friend interrupted her and said; "hmmm, it is a strike; ain't it?"

I am always tickled by her witty comebacks; especially the ones that border disrespect. Another; episode was while we were teenagers; our math teacher advised her not to play games with me in school because my "bread was buttered;" my Sister retorted with this, "Well, if that's the case my biscuits are jammed!" I love her! She and I lived almost the same lives as teenagers; mom had moved to the US and Dad was a drill sergeant. She is the only one who ever understood how that felt.

She is still alive; thank God but I guess I needed to share what she means to me. I speak of her here because she introduced me to one of the coolest, strangest sisters I will ever know. I think I mostly felt that way because she was very religious and I enjoyed challenging her beliefs. It would get her all flustered; but she stood on her beliefs and defended them faithfully.

She was a fighter; no she was a champion. For the brief time I had been blessed with her in my life I learned a lot from her. She decided for herself that she had to live the life she desired to live; even if that went against all she was raised to believe.

She endured great suffering in the 3 years we had each other; she died a cruel death at the hands of her abuser and I vow to keep my fight to bring awareness of domestic violence and win in her honor.

This brings lumps to my throat; so I'll speak of two sisters I met through Poetry. One I met in my early years of poetry and performance. She stood on a stage, the only female in an all-male group and she belted out prose and notes and for all the years I've known her; her "Light," it's so real and many times her voice has brought the spirit of "Harriet" back to life.

The other sister; her last words to me was "Keep doing what you're doing; I'm proud of you." This was a month before she left us to move on to a more "Infinite" realm; and the night of my event "Stop In the Name of Love" where she had performed a very powerful piece with another gifted poet. Sometimes I still hear her voice reminding me of how many "Dandelions" are left to be saved.

Clarity shared her "Momma" with me; that was one of the greatest gifts she could give to me.

"Momma" was the epitome of an earthly angel. She just accepted you for who you are and until you proved differently; she loved and respected you as who you presented yourself to be. She mothered me in a way I will never forget.

She gave my child and I a place to live and treated us like we were a part of her. In fact; she made us a part of her. She gently admonished me when I was wrong; fiercely pushed me when she saw great possibilities and sat with me whenever I just needed to be in her presence. She still does that in my dreams. She didn't have much; but she helped plenty and she shared her little with many.

I am blessed that her spirit is still in fellowship with me today.

My dear friend "Iron" had limited mobility in one leg and none in one arm; but he worked 5 days a week and was as self-sufficient as any of us with normal function. He battled seizures; yet he enjoyed all that life would allow him and he fought to live.

He proved to me that I could make do with what I have or make what I have do for me. I love him for being the fighter he was.

I grieve many; but I mention just these few because they are all vessels who allowed themselves to be used to help ferment me.

"Then he called the bridegroom aside and said, "Everyone brings out the choice wine first and then the cheaper wine after the guests have had too much to drink;"

It was my English teacher in the St. Michael's Secondary School of Barbados who introduced me to what I call my Essence. My friend "Motivation" encouraged me daily to write and my daughter's birth bore life to my "Inspiration."

Every mother has a story to tell about raising a child; many of us share the same story. We speak of love, fear, fight, flight, pride, patience, joy, prayers, tears, humility and faith. Some people say they loved their child from his or her first breath; I knew I was in love the day I accepted I was carrying our future. She would be beautiful, strong and graceful.

I called her "Butterfly" because my Doctor asked me if I had been feeling the baby move around and I told him no; I just kept getting Butterflies in my stomach. He laughed and then allowed my sister "Victory" and I to hear her heartbeat. "Victory" had traveled from Florida to be there for that experience; she's always there for the best ones.

She is my big sister and a Libra and I love her more for who she is. We don't talk as much now, but whenever we do it is jewel dropping time. Today Victory calls my baby "Scooter;" that suits her too.

I went into labor during a snow storm; a heavy one. Her god father and I walked 6 blocks before we could get a cab. The nurse at the hospital told me to go back home and I laughed at her. See, what she didn't know was that I had a bet to win and a promise to keep to her godfather "J.P" that I would have her on that day; his birthday.

I had 7 people in the hospital with me; 4 had medical background and took turns overseeing my labor. At delivery time it was the Matriarch who entered that room with me giving advice all along the way.

I thought I was prepared; I even perfected what the doctor later called my "T.V cry." Her heart beat had decelerated and as they rushed me into the delivery room I wished I had said YES to drugs.

Giving birth is real; the feeling of bringing something you've created and nurtured over months into existence. The soul searching it inspires and the memories it creates. The tears; many rivers flowed from my eyes as I navigated through many troubled waters; a lot of times due to my decisions and choices.

I believe *"sometimes God lets us trouble the waters so we can witness Him make them still again."*

The way I see it now; I had to birth my daughter if I would ever be inspired to pursue and discover my purpose.

Many think I am over protective of her but they don't understand that protecting her is protecting my dreams. She is my Muse; my greatest testimony and sweetest victory.

I remember her waiting for me to get home from work one day. I was frustrated and had sat outside smoking a cigarette to blow off the steam I brought home from the law firm. I had many of those days and so I tried not to bring that negativity into my home. The difference that day was her sitting outside the elevator when I stepped on to our floor.

I asked her what was wrong and she said she just felt like waiting for me out there. She hugs and kisses me and begins to tell me how she knows I feel bad about not being able to provide what was considered luxury items to a teenager.

All her friends were into brands and had high end cell phones and I-pods; she had the basics. She went on to tell me that though her friends had all that material stuff she had me. She said "I can come to you with anything and you talk it out. You trust me and I trust you and even my friends think you're cool enough to talk to."

"Mom; that makes me the ***PRIVILEDGED*** one."

Her friends; a group of young ladies I have the pleasure of calling "My girls" were affectionately known as my "JEWELS" until they all entered high school and now they are my "YOUNG QUEENS RISING".

That was initially the name I used for the group of High School girls I mentored in a High School in Brooklyn; another blessing *Poetry* brought my way.

Queen of Cool

When I step into a room people glance for a moment
And then they catch my vibe
They see a sister enhanced with pride
A woman with a confident stride
A mother with a satisfied glow
I'm a lady
Oh yeah, they know
They know that I live by the rules
The rules that make me
The Queen of Cool.

Class is in session Sisters, gather round
Let me tell you how I did this
Let me break it down
See, I put myself out there
Called myself trying to play the game
All I achieved was a reputation
I ruined my name
I recognize early that things were going all wrong
That my actions, caused reactions
With which I could not be down
I looked at myself in the mirror
All I saw was pain and disgrace
Child when I tell you
I didn't recognize my own face
I took a mental picture

Took myself back to soul school
Self Love was my major
And I graduated, the Queen of Cool.

Life broke my ignorance down by steps
First I lost my soul
My spirituality up and left
I was no longer whole
False passion and deception
Plagued my being
I disliked the image of me I was seeing
Then about life I no longer cared
I was overpowered by my fears

One day my 3rd eye opened up
And I was finally able to see
I had to search among the ruins of my Queendom
In efforts to find me
I rose up tall and dusted off
The residue of my past
The ghost of that experience
I had seen for the last

So, Sisters that's my story line
I now live by the golden rule
No more jiving
I'm just vibing
That's why I'm the Queen of Cool.

I could have stayed in the cesspool of drama and negativity that my life had become; but I would have missed out on so much. Instead I have decided to treat it like a mud bath. I sit in it just long enough to allow the nature of each experience to saturate and when I come out the impurities are left behind:

> - I've left behind the disappointments
> - I've left behind the mistakes
> - I've left behind the pain
> - I've left behind the failures
> - I've left behind the abuse
> - I've left behind the ridicule
> - I've left behind the loss
> - I've left behind the struggle
> - I've left behind the abandonment
> - I've left behind the insecurity
> - I've left behind the negativity
> - I've left behind the negative people
> - I've left behind the dream snatchers
> - I've left behind the tears
> - I've left behind the fears
> - I've left behind the uncertainty
> - I've left the past behind

Purpose

She was a soul burdened by fear and rejection
A shell of the woman she was created to be
She was a battered bird whose wings had been broken
An apple that had fallen too far from the tree

She was angry, broken and bitter
Her words fierce like venomous lava on queue
She fought just to prove she's no quitter
She was repulsed at the words, "I love you"

See for some time I
I mean, she
Ok, we had a battle going on inside of me
My mind was a field of pure misery,
Uncertainty, negativity, devastation
Everything I conceived led to destruction
My Midas touch turned nothing to gold
I found myself in a place that was lonely and cold
Where darkness was the blanket that covered me
Somewhere in the fog a voice cried out "rescue me"

I was too weak to even care about my destiny
Self love?
Empowerment?
That was all foreign to me
A worthless, wasted soul is all I had known myself to be

I had heard it

I felt it

I consumed it

I received it

No one would ever believe in me

I wanted to fall into an eternal sleep

Noted as a seed which was planted in barren land

Deep

Somewhere deep in that mud bath of pity

My soul extracted purity

After the blood bath

My soul was granted liberty

I was divinely baptized in a fire

That blazed the way for me to be free

A lineage of Kings and Queens

Their lives are the thread count of my tapestry

I am an upgrade

A Rebirth

A sure heir of royalty

And it all started with me, believing in me

I dived back in that pool

And rescued my destiny

And she brought with her my passion

Which, summoned my inner diva

And now I wear my purpose like a couture fashion

I now stomp this stage with an inspired pump

Head up

Back straight

Can't keep my crown on if I slump

What was once my runway

Is now just another stage

Inspiration fuels my drive

Which was once being fostered by rage

I have evolved into who God created me to be

My passion is my purpose

My purpose is my poetry

And it all started with me believing in me

I am Empress Poetry©

"but you have saved the best till now."

There was a time I thought that age 42 meant all things had to be in place in my life or it was a bust. Times I felt that I should be in a healthy relationship, great career and financially endowed. Time for my child to stop seeing me hustle; and then I almost lost my home.

Despite all of the struggle I managed to maintain my home; a sure way I can testify that GOD WILL DO IT IF WE BELIEVE AND TRUST IN HIM.

This last battle was rough; one day the landlord's lawyer yelled at me in the middle of the conference room; "NO! Stop fighting us! WE ARE TRYING TO GET RID OF YOU!" This was after I had taken my case to the Appellate court to shut down the decision of the lower judge who I'm sure was being greased.

I found that ironic since he had not seen me approaching him and his paralegal; he had his back to me. I had not identified myself as yet because his paralegal saw me so I just served him the documents. This tiny clone of the devil who once told me I was despicable and I should pay my rent and not my phone bill; was the same vessel used to prove to me that this battle is not mine.

I am a vessel being used to demonstrate God's amazing grace. I am a survivor, a fighter, a conqueror; but that's all because God stands in at the harshest of attacks.

The day this gross man called me despicable was the same day I received a letter from child support threatening my incarceration if I did not show up for a case to listen to my child's father defend why he should get a downward modification from $25.00 a month. I wanted to quit; but then I remembered what that hermit crab of a lawyer said; *"WE ARE TRYING TO GET RID OF YOU!"*

"Who is <u>WE</u>?"

That day it became clear that I needed to write this book; share this part of the journey. Keeping it honest; poverty inspired me to get off my pen. Use my gifts to build my wealth; keep baby girl on top of the hills of Baltimore pursuing her dreams as a Morganite; keep the roof over our heads, food on the table; keep the lights and gas on; keep the epicenter of our village secure.

I also have to admit that I knew it had to be written so others understand there is purpose in our journey.

If I had not lost my dad; I would have never found the strength to stand on my own.

If I had not been a single mother; I would never have known how deeply a child needs both parents. I also would not have experience the love and support that we received from the many who repeatedly have come to our rescue.

I would not have known how deep Sisterhood could run

Or how exceptional a responsible black man is.

If I had not survived domestic violence I would not have had the chance to rescue the ones I have. I would have selfishly kept my story locked in notebooks and on hard drives. I would not have found my voice.

If I had not been an undocumented resident; I would not have gained such a deep appreciation for the hustle. Despite my credentials; suitable jobs are hard to find if you are not straight in this place. I also would not truly appreciate the hard work and determination it takes to survive here.

Had it not been for the ill treatment, the tears, the betrayal, those who took advantage; the suffering; I would not be able to see the blessings.

If it had not been for it all; I would not have seen God's plans for me. I would not have recognized how deeply he loves me. I would not have discovered ME!

That moment when....YOUR PURPOSE WAKES YOU UP!!!!!

It is one thing to SPEAK about FAITH; You are on an ENTIRE OTHER level when it comes to EXERCISING IT!!!!!

Life can be seen as "not fair" sometimes; one battle ends and while you think the dust is clearing from that one, it's actually another kicking up. It just doesn't seem FAIR! But, YOU KEEP FIGHTING; tired and worn. Feeling defeated while refusing to ACCEPT defeat....SO YOU FIGHT! You fight because living in YOU is a FIGHTER!!!!

You may not "win" every round, but you are STILL IN THE RING! Pound for pound you take a hit but you hit back. You bob and weave to avoid the swings you see coming; you may fall from the unexpected one....BUT YOU STAND BACK UP! YOU STAND because living in YOU is a CHAMPION!!!!!

YOU may cry, especially when you pray. You want to ask why; but won't because you already know. These battles and test are not meant to defeat YOU; instead they are your OBSTACLE COURSE! Designed for ONLY YOU to navigate through; for YOU to gain KNOWLEDGE of SELF! For YOU to gain WISDOM! For YOU to gain STRENGTH! FOR YOU TO CONQUER!

Everyone you meet is on their own OBSTACLE COURSE, EVERY ONE OF THEM IS ALSO TRYING TO WIN THEIR RACE!

Some you will see fall and you will stop to help them STAND. Some will see you fall and do the same for you. Though we all have our separate courses; it's important to acknowledge we share the same track.

So expect that though you will lift others up; others will see you fall and run past you. Some will run OVER you and others will watch it all go down. DO NOT BE DISCOURAGED; GET UP, DUST YOURSELF OFF AND NAVIGATE ON!!!! It is a part of THE RACE!

WE ALL WANT TO WIN!

I am in the race of my life! Sometimes it feels like I've completed a lap, yet I'm still at the start waiting for the gun. I've had dreams about this and feel this way NOW!

But, I've come to learn that I can worry about my problems and allow the pre-race jitters to consume me to the point where I'm frozen at the start. Allow the shenanigans of fellow runners to distract me to the point where I'm late out the gate. Or, put my head down and LISTEN! LISTEN FOR THE GO!!!!!

I know now that falling down is not the end of the race. I know that helping others to stand will not slow me down or give them a chance to get ahead of me. I know that being run over doesn't make me a loser; but that running over another DOES! I know I WILL WIN MY RACE!

I know some will have already made it to their VICTORY and will stand on their pedestal too consumed by acknowledging their OWN; to salute the accomplishments of another. I still SALUTE YOU! (They will also forget who helped keep them on track.)

I know some will reach their VICTORY and wait at the finish line to celebrate TOGETHER! I know some will stay in their lane and leave room for me to catch up in mine.

Some will wait for me as I wait for others and together we will cross. (Probably in a flashmob/ conga line kinda way)

I know it doesn't matter what POSITION we finish this race in; what matters is HOW IT WAS RUN! Remember each of US has our OWN obstacle course to run, how you FINISH IS WHAT MAKES THE WINNER! THERE IS A WINNER LIVING IN YOU!

I AM NOT JUST RUNNING A RACE; I AM BUILDING STRENGTH AND DEVELOPING MUSCLES! I AM JUMPING HURDLES, SPRINTING WHEN I HAVE TO; BUT DOING IT AT MY PACE. I FALL, GET UP, REACH BACK, REACH FORWARD; I EVEN SLOW DOWN TO CATCH MY BREATH. ONE THING I DO NOT...CANNOT...AND WILL NOT DO; IS STOP!!!!!! And though the finish line seems far away; I AM EXERCISING FAITH, TAKING IT ONE LAP AT A TIME!

I KNOW WITH GOD ALL THINGS ARE POSSIBLE; WITH GOD I WILL WIN MY RACE!!!!

As I approach age 42; I know that God uses many vessels and chooses grapes from my experiences, both sweet and sour. He has taken me; a once empty vessel, repaired my cracks and filled me with such joy it overflows.

The tears I once cried serves as the waters He has taken and turned into wine. It's not over; nope, my journey has just begun.

I hope reading this book gives you as much inspiration as writing it has given me. I am no longer living in shadows; hiding that which is me. I will still stumble; but I know now I can't stay down if I fall.

I have nieces and nephews who depend on me being who I am to them; I must show by example how life can give you lemons and we sometimes may choose to make lemonade OR we can sell those lemons; buy some grapes and make our own wine/ champagne.

I must stand for my sisters; and fight alongside my brothers.

I must take these tests and turn them into testimonies.

Many never knew how the vessel got cracked; some didn't care where the waters came from. Others drank the wine without considering its depletion; and they did not care about the grapes. Some see me as a cheap; or devalued brand….BUT I INTEND TO LIVE AS A TESTIMONY THAT MY GOD…. *HE SAVES THE BEST FOR LAST.*

Exercising Prayer

Dear Lord, I stretch my hands above my head
Inhaling breaths of life
Thanking you for delivering me
From all my stress and strife
You've rescued me from certain death
And saved my soul from sin
As I exhale, I release
All negativity within
I sway my arms from side to side
Giving honor and praise to you
For when times get rough and rugged
You always bring me through
Though sometimes my breath is labored
I still lunge towards the goal
I've learned that I must pace myself
It's healthy for my soul
I bow my head and bend my back
As I reach for my toes
Saying prayers and asking mercy
I need delivery from my woes
I used to squat in hiding
Did crunches from all the pain
I could not believe just how much
Weight of the world I had gained
I curl my arms as I receive
My blessings from above

I feel my heart rate increase
As I recognize your love
And sometimes Lord, the race gets tough
But I still sprint to the finish line
For you said that when I get there
Victory will be mine
So I'll crunch and run and squat and lunge
I'll stretch and curl and spin
I'm readying myself for the battle
And with your help I'll win
Father God, I stretch my arms to you
And inhale a breath of life
For as long as I keep this routine
I know I'll win the prize, Amen

Untitled

She swallowed her pride

So she could savor the flavor of what she thought was love on her tongue

But she was wrong

And after; all she could taste was bitter

Her thoughts and dreams tainted by doses of deception and pain

Experience was the meaning gained by taking it as medication

Meant to hurt the spirit but strengthens the soul

A brutal form of humiliation; yet she's growing

The roots of her heart were buried where pain dwells

She planted her trust too and now her secrets its aroma tells

A pungent smell that leaves her nauseous and infected

Like a parasite; all her good energy it collected

Then deposited her like diarrhea

Nothing; nothing can be done

Nothing can be said, are the words that most of her loved ones said to; and for her

So she looked from her broken spirit to her Father instead

And prayed; "fix me."

Smiles on her face would ride; though deep inside she was dying

Through tears and laughs she released her past while reminding herself to keep trying

Never give up

From her bended knees God heard her pleas and filled her cup

She's not perfect but what is; is the fact that she knows that

So she does the best she can with what she has

Preserved supplies of determination shelved until on demand

Because she knows she can

They are her spice of life; comeback is her brand

She could remain broken and battered; but that would be her choice

Her cries would become silent tears

Because she lost her voice and gave up her power

But she knows now it's during the birthing hours

That's when the contractions become fierce

So she takes a deep breath and breaks sound barriers on her exhale

Her release is unexpected so some will be impaled by her return

She'll cross over bridges that others had burned to keep her on the other side

Her faith walks on water as she floats with the tide

Her waves are tidal

Her essence; it just continues to flow

Inspired by a Broken Shell

I am but one shell on a shore where thousands more are also
shattered pieces of their future self

Sitting still in hot sands waiting for the occasional wave of joy to
cool the heat of life

Though parts of me are missing my beauty glistens in the light of
the Sun

Kisses on the wind reminds me I am a chosen one and so I must
stand out

Outstanding trials and tribulations because it must be done to
promote my growth

Withstanding storms and dry seasons bares experience this I
know

So I endure

With faith and determination even when I find myself on the
floor of a cesspool

Or times I find myself swimming with clown fish in a school

But hey, now my freestyle is a beautiful butterfly stroke and
that's cool

Waters wash over my shadow self as waves crash to the shores

Taking back energy that burdens me no more

Leaving me in cleaner surroundings

On solid grounds I'm standing

No longer sinking sands

No longer placing my trust in man but loving all the way

Proving it in every move and every word I say; it's all I have left

Many frolic around me conjuring death

But my Spirit will not die
And these tears; these tears I cry
Will flow into the sea; and I

I will still be
One shell on a shore where thousands more are also shattered
I'm just trying to pull it together piece by Peace.

Sometimes

Sometimes....I feel like a testimony stuck in a Praiser's throat

Like, the option that makes the decision easier for a smoker not to smoke

Or the second before the celebration as a new year enters at midnight's stroke

The subliminal behind a cruel joke or the joke itself

Sometimes, I feel like the secret no one wants to tell

Those times make me want to holla; they make me want to yell

And hear Job's wife's advice but that wouldn't be very smart

Sometimes I feel like that last beat of a failing heart

Like the space between a question and it's mark

Sometimes I feel like the bag that holds the extra parts of a new toy

Life sometimes makes me feel undeserving of joy

Like the epitome of sorrow

Like the hope for sunny skies even though the forecast calls a rainy tomorrow

A lotto number off by one

Like the mushy part of an under cooked honey bun

Sometimes, instead of fight; I truly want to run

But at no time can I accept this as my fate

Not when I know God has for me a purpose and I just need to wait

For Him to move

For Him to lift these sanctions and prove that I am Victory.

Lioness Arise

Your roar has been minimized to a purr

Darkness deafens your light

Your dreams have been stolen by the fear that nurtures your plight

Lioness, Arise

Rise like the beautiful sun that greets you from the skies

Let your light shine so bright it burns your enemies eyes

Show your strength in all that you do

Release the weaknesses of your past

And allow the Creator to use you

Use your jewel, filled with wisdom

Overflowing knowledge from the crown

Show the world why you should never be held down

You are a lioness, now rise

Your dreams and purpose deflect the threats of your demise

Traps have been set, there's false premise of promise

Delusions of grandeur, all sealed with a Judas kiss

You've been broken, we all have

You've been lied to, so have I

Dwelling deep inside of us is what we need to survive

DIG, Discover Inner Goals

Find what you need in order to free your soul

Let your destiny be your prey

Stalk elevation, everyday

You have to fight for the honor of your pride

Stop licking your wounds and allowing yourself to be pushed aside

Your cubs are watching and so is the rest of your lair

As a natural born leader

You must devour your fears

Don't become endangered in this jungle we call life

You are a queen, Lioness Arise.

The following are the thoughts and realities that gave me the drive to complete this book. Their dates and content document the journey I took while carrying it; from PASSION TO PURPOSE.

May 20, 2015

Today my daughter comes home from her FIRST year of college and I am excited and humbled and EXTREMELY BLESSED!

I remember the stress and anxiety that started right about this time last year when I had to acknowledge that certain things I needed to have in place by that time were not even in existence; I had lost my job the month prior and our options became limited. I panicked, cried and prayed. SHE WORKED ON GRADUATING!

MISSION ACCOMPLISH

As time grew close to her leaving, we were being denied loans and the amount of tuition seemed like a mountain. I created a gofundme account and received $300.00 (THANK YOU TO THOSE CONTRIBUTORS! ♥) I produced shows and performed at events; did editing jobs and prayed. SHE WORKED ON WINNING SCHOLARSHIPS!

MISSION ACCOMPLISH

The time was nigh, she was safe on campus and THEN the storms came! I got evicted from the same apartment 3 times; (PRAISE GOD, I'M STILL HERE); lights were cut off; still no stable job; plans for life changing events that would have made it all better were cancelled or abruptly ended; projects I had planned to keep us afloat got delayed. I cried, and fought and prayed. SHE WORKED ON PASSING HER CLASSES!

MISSION ACCOMPLISH

And here we are today; she's on her way home.....first year complete!!!! Scholarship applications in! Grants applied for! Classes for fall 2015 chosen! Member of the national leadership and success society! High school dance instructor! MSU ambassador! No student loans!

MISSION ACCOMPLISH

I write this post amid tears of praise because if I never knew God; He made himself known to us during these times. I felt at times that I was shadow boxing with demons, but he tagged in and sent me to my corner.

He planted people there who each played a role in helping us achieve this victory! They cheered us on, wiped my tears, prayed with and for us and aided us in many, many other ways.

Donations, rides, rental cars, microwaves, school supplies, books, scholarship information; etc.

GOD IS NOT DEAD! HE HEARS OUR PRAYER, SEES OUR TEARS AND CONQUERS OUR FEARS!

He uses the emptiest of vessels to make the most beautiful noise!

I was shattered into several pieces during this year! Had nothing more times than I had anything! I had emotional breakdowns; moments of surrender; failure; crushed dreams; malicious acts; weak moments; legal battles; physical, mental and emotional fights; ruined friendships; deception; times I sat silently and just let things happen even when inside my head I was screaming "get up, speak out"; moments I found myself thinking flight....not fight! Moments of tantrums; shame, fear; fears and more fears! But we made it!

Her absentee father looked me in my face and challenged me with the following words after refusing to help her through college; just as he has all her life......
"You've always made it happen; let me see you do it this time!"
Even him God used as a vessel because he lit fire under my motivation with that!

Father God; I thank you for using me to show your miraculous works and your presence in our lives. I thank you for each challenge, each denial, each betrayal, each fall, each fallout, each battle, every storm!

I look back on this first year with mixed emotions for there are some I wish to thank who are no longer here; so I thank you for them. I thank you for those whose seasons in my life are over; for those who have stood with me through the storms. Thank you for not allowing bitterness or self pity to overcome me! For seeing me through depression and for giving me the following message to whomever it is for....

I love you lord; you've heard my cries! You've used me to prove that even the biggest fears can be conquered by our faith in you. You've shown me that even when I think I can't do it I can! You've given me love, delivered directly from you and through your earth bound angels. You've protected me. You showed me my value even when I stopped believing in me and allowed the wicked actions of others to cause me to question my worth. You made me fight!

When I had no money, you cancelled debts! When I had no options; you solved the issues! Even shackled by the chains that hold me captive in my life; you have allowed me advance. I praise you! Now and forever more! Amen.

For whomever it is that needs to know.....God is real!!!! He brought us through!! He will do it! He did it and is still doing it for us!!!

KEEP FIGHTING! KEEP PRAYING! KEEP PRAISNG! KEEP THE FAITH! WOW!

MISSION ACCOMPLISH

Tuesday, June 30, 2015

I'm just gonna take this lesson and share it!

Someone right now is crying their last hope out. Someone is battling giving up! Someone thinks GOD is too busy or can't hear their cries! SOMEONE WANTS TO GIVE UP!!!!!

I'm telling you....DON'T!

Don't QUIT

Don't YOU QUIT

Don't your let your DREAMS die in the hands of people who envy you for having them.

Don't let those who have MORE; treat you as LESS

Don't allow others to pull you into their misery

Don't let your PAST consume YOU!

DON'T. ...DON'T. ...DON'T LET YOUR SITUATION ERASE YOU!!!!

I sit here typing this message on a phone that is about to be disconnected;

Marshals are due to arrive any day now!

No job; kid in college, with an inactive father taking me to court to fight paying $25.00 a month in support. Engagement to one of the GREATEST gifts I've had in my life....BROKEN

Total deadbeats treating me like I am NOTHING!

And an entire village who sees me as their refuge!!!!!

I know....some of you are asking why I'm airing my business;

I AM because it's my story to tell and if this is the ONLY PURPOSE GOD HAS FOR ME.....IT HAS BEEN FULFILLED.

I tell it because one day we will look back at it in amazement of the work god is performing through me and we will all say ....WOW!!!!!

I tell it; because I recently lost a friend, sister, LIGHT in my life because she didn't SHARE!

I share it because as I sit here crying my life away; crunched into a fetal position; with no clue of what comes next.........I STILL BELIEVE THAT GOD.....HE KNOWS BEST!!!!!!!

So don't cry for me UNIVERSE; because GOD......HE HAS A PLAN!!!!!!!! Talk about me...laugh if you must! God knows some of you needed the comedy; makes your stuff seem LIGHT!

TAKE from it what you need..... I LIVE MY LIFE TO PLEASE GOD! I'm not always pleasing to Him but.....HE LOVES ME STILL!

So, the next chapter seems uncertain but HE'S NOT DONE WITH ME YET!!!!!
My POETRY and the LOVE of my VILLAGE....SUSTAINS MY FAITH IN GOD!!!!

Pray for me, as I pray for you and be ENCOURAGED.....IT'S NOT OVER!!!!!
I LOVE YOU

Friday, July 10, 2015

LORD JESUS YOU ARE MY LIGHT AND JOY!!!!! YOU
ARE MY DEFINITION!!!

This morning I confessed to myself that over the past 6 months I
have been feeling like a QUESTION MARK; "A SYMBOL
THAT INDICATES A QUESTION OR QUERY;"

I had been slowly shrinking to a PERIOD....FULL STOP...END
OF THE ROAD!!!! "A SYMBOL THAT IS USED LIKE A
KNIFE TO CUT SENTENCES TO THE REQUIRED
LENGTH!"

I have been living like a CONJUNCTION; specifically the noun
IF... I FELT "used to introduce an exclamatory clause, indicating
a wish" as in: "If they had only come earlier!"

I was A POSSIBILITY....living under CONDITIONS AND
STIPULATION: as in: "There will be no IFs, ands, or buts in this
matter."
And a lot of times it inserted thoughts of uncertainty; DOUBTS:
as in: "There are too many "IFs" in this plan of yours."

But......God has REDEFINED MY DEFINITION AND MY
PUNCTUATIONS!!!!

He has allowed me to come through jumbled situations in my life
like A SEMICOLON; A SYMBOL USED TO JOIN TWO OR
MORE IDEAS/PARTS AND EACH ARE GIVEN "EQUAL
POSITION OR RANK"

That's how I manage to link my bad experiences to the invaluable lessons I learn from them. That's how I am now able to prioritize people and situations; based on POSITION AND RANK!

I DO NOT have it all together; I've questioned my purpose, my existence, my value, my decisions, my actions and a lot of times; TOO OFTEN FOR MY LIKING, my life has been halted to a PERIOD.

Plans that were FOR SURE have been cut short; way before my sentence reached its required length. Many of my sentences are still jumbled and many more are COMPLEX!

A COMPLEX SENTENCE "contains one main clause or independent clause and at least one subordinate clause or dependent clause"

EXAMPLE: "Although I am TIRED (subordinate clause), I want to ACHIEVE MY GOALS (main clause)."

Today, I feel like an EXCLAMATION MARK!!! A SYMBOL THAT INDICATES STRONG FEELINGS OR HIGH VOLUME!

Today, I strongly BELIEVE that *IT IS MY PURPOSE TO LIVE MY LIFE IN HIGH VOLUME!!!!*

Today, I know that GOD is the only one who can put a period at the end of my sentence because he alone is the author and finisher of my life....AND HE'S NOT DONE WITH ME YET!!!!

August 19, 2015

In a few days my baby girl heads back out to begin her sophomore year in college; I am so blessed to witness her growth.

As my "BUTTERFLY" prepares for YEAR TWO.... back to her cocoon where she sheds old thoughts and behavior and return each time renewed; I feel more butterflies!

For as she gracefully dances from stage to stage like flowers in a garden; I watch her drawn only to what she likes in their sweet, alluring fragrance.

Her journey beautifies my world! I am so in honor to be in her presence; awed by God's work in and through her.

I've made many mistakes and paid for them cruelly; but I am so grateful to God and to her for showing me that my mistakes do not make ME! That true love comes unconditionally and though times get rough and things seem impossible, that their LOVE makes it all bearable.

Just as the Creator has aligned and assigned angels in our lives; I pray this book serves as another way to help someone see....YES GOD WILL DO IT!!!!!

GO head baby, deep breaths
It's just a bigger stage to display your choreography
Pop, lock and rock your way along the path to reach your destiny
Steady steps and perfect form sometimes may fail
Just pivot, pas de chat and pirouette
Plie´ and prayer when things seem to block your way
As God carries you, Petit Saut and Pique´
Go head Baby take a deep breath
It's just a bigger stage
After your best execution let God do the rest
Just stay in faith
And also stay in character
Praise dance in the face of danger
Jazz fingers to the world
Because that little girl is now La Prima Ballerina
Arabesque and display your extensions
Be clear, cou-de-pied your intentions
Stay devant, and let others fall into positions
This is your dance
So even if you join a conga-line
Be the head not the tail and you'll be fine
If you look into the audience I'm sure you'll find
Your biggest supporters are here to be your spine
So go head baby, take a deep breath
It's just bigger stage to display your technique
Let the wind of inspiration lift you off your feet
May our love fuel your determination
We will always honor you with a standing ovation

So dance, BABY.....DANCE!!!!!

I wasn't sure how to end this book, but I decided to end it with a dedication to my inspiration. I love you Butterfly; thank you for choosing me.

ABOUT THE AUTHOR

NOTHING WITHOUT HELP FROM GOD

I am more than a conqueror through Christ who strengthens me. That is why..... I LIVE, I WRITE, I AM!

Who defines the essence of a modern day heroine with authoritative poise, encased in earthy beauty, eloquently delivered in a socially conscious packaging that makes audiences and discerning poetically stoked critics take notice everywhere?

Meet performance artist, poetic activist, author, motivational speaker and mother EMPRESS POETRY. Barbados born and Brooklyn, New York bred; this culturally rich and diverse combo gives her a creatively unique edged color palate and a horizon- wide canvas. EMPRESS POETRY cleverly weaves language and molds character through the power of the pen. Her signature performance poetry captures the delicate intricacies of life. These natural, God-given creative abilities were evident early on. Today, EMPRESS dynamically brings uplifting messages of self-discovery, empowerment, and healing through her God given gift of writing poetry and prose to every onstage/offstage encounter.

As author of Impressions of a Poet, Footnotes of My Journey(c)2011, she has documented some of her life lessons through prose. Her best assignment is her teenaged daughter, who she credits as the best inspiration she's ever had. With God as her guide, Empress keeps confidence in her stride as she stomps in her PURPOSE. She is also included in the anthology Wordplay, Words Are Our Canvas(c)2012.